Manners Are Important for You and Me

Written by
Todd Snow

Illustrated by
Carrie Hartman

Maren Green Publishing, Inc.
Oak Park Heights, Minnesota

For my well-mannered daughter, Greta. You always inspire me.
Love, Dad

To my mom and dad, for teaching me all my manners.
Love, Carrie

Ages 3 and up

Maren Green Publishing, Inc.
5525 Memorial Avenue North, Suite 6
Oak Park Heights, MN 55082
Toll-free 800-287-1512

Text copyright © 2007 Todd Snow
Illustrations copyright © 2007 Carrie Hartman

Library of Congress Control Number: 2007926552

Edited by Pamela Espeland
Text set in Garamond Pro
Illustrations created using pastels on Reeves paper

First Edition October 2007
10 9 8 7 6 5 4 3 2 1
Manufactured in China

ISBN 978-1-934277-04-1 (pbk.)

www.marengreen.com

Manners are important for you and me.
Why are manners important?
Read on and see.

Manners show we have respect
for people and things.

Manners help us be polite
with the kindness they bring.

Manners let others know how we want to be treated.
Manners make the world a happier place to be greeted.

When there's something you want,
it's best to say "Please."
But do you know what to say
right after you sneeze?*

Try not to let that sneeze fly off like a breeze.
Quick! Bend your head and aim for your sleeve!

* Say "Excuse me!" after you sneeze.

When you get a present from your family or friend,
say "Thank you" and write a note to send.

People speak many languages, depending on where they're from.
English, Spanish, Danish, Greek, and Japanese are some.

You can use two kinds of voices.
Do you wonder what they are?
Your *inside** voice when inside and near.

* *quiet*

Your *outside** voice when outside and far.

* *LOUD!*

In a restaurant, when you go out to eat,
use your *inside* voice
and stay in your seat.

What goes in your lap?*
Not a toy, game, or ball.
(Hint: It's something to catch
any food that might fall.)

* A napkin goes in your lap.

Take small bites and close your mouth when you chew.
Say "Please" if you want something,
then "Thank you."

But before you say anything, swallow your food.
Showing others what's in your mouth is rude!

When you see someone you know,
smile and say "Hello!"
Ask "How are you?"
to let your caring show.

That's a good way to meet and make friends, too.
Then learn more about them by asking "What's new?"

When you phone a friend to come over to play,
manners can help you know what to say.

Instead of just blurting "Can I talk to Luke?"
say...

* Fill in with your name.

If you want to play with something different and new,
ask first if it doesn't belong to you.

When you're with new friends you're trying to make,
remember that it's not polite to just take.

Do you know how to shake hands? Hold, don't crush.
If the person says OW! you're squeezing too much!

When people leave
to go on their way,
say a friendly "Goodbye!"
or "Have a nice day!"

It's great to talk with friends about all kinds of things,
  like stories, plans, and happy memories.
But it's not polite to whisper when others are near.

They might feel left out, sad,
or mad if they can't hear.

When others are speaking, wait till they're through.
Jumping in is interrupting, and it's not polite to do.

What if someone interrupts you, even in fun?

Say "Excuse me.
I was speaking,
and I wasn't quite done."

When you play tag or soccer or any kind of game,
it's fun to be the winner and enjoy your fame.

But good sports are kind
to those who lose, too.
Saying "Nice job!" or "Great game!"
is the polite thing to do.

Now share your good manners with everyone you know.
Don't be shy or hide them. Let your manners show!

When we all use manners, this is what we'll see:
A world that's gentle, polite, and kind—a better place to be.

Also Available from Maren Green Publishing

Manners Are Important Board Book *By Todd Snow, illustrated by Carrie Hartman.* A child's first book about manners. Simple words and colorful pictures cover the basics of polite behavior. *Board book, full color, 6" x 6", 32 pages. Ages Baby–Preschool.* **MG104 $6.99**

ISBN 978-1-934277-05-8

ISBN 978-1-934277-00-3

Feelings to Share from A to Z *By Todd and Peggy Snow, illustrated by Carrie Hartman.* Help children understand and express their feelings. This book gives kids the words they need to tell you how they feel, from A (Awesome) to Z (Zany) and every letter in between. It's a lively, colorful alphabet of emotions, fun to read aloud, talk about, and hear. *Paperback, full color, 8" x 8", 32 pages. Ages 3 & up.* **MG101 $9.99**

Feelings to Share Board Book *By Todd and Peggy Snow, illustrated by Carrie Hartman.* A child's first book about feelings. Simple words and colorful pictures help little ones understand and talk about how they feel. *Board book, full color, 6" x 6", 24 pages. Ages Baby—Preschool.* **MG102 $6.99**

ISBN 978-1-934277-01-0

162 Stickers

Feelings Stickers. All 26 feelings from the *Feelings to Share from A to Z* paperback on colorful stickers to wear and share, plus write-on stickers for expressing more feelings. Set includes five 8 1/2" x 11" sheets of 27 stickers each and a full sheet of write-on stickers: 162 in all. Each is 2" x 1", removable and safe for use on clothing. *All ages.* **MG114 $4.99**

w w w . m a r e n g r e e n . c o m

5525 Memorial Avenue North, Suite 6 • Oak Park Heights, MN 55082
phone 800-287-1512 • 651-439-4500 • fax 651-439-4532 • email orders@marengreen.com